RESCUED! ANIMAL ESCA

Vanished in the Hurricane

DOLPHIN RESCUE!

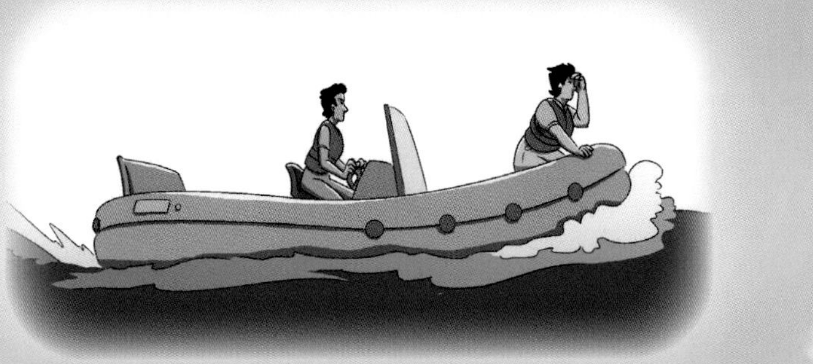

By James Buckley Jr.

Illustrated by Kerstin LaCross

BEARPORT PUBLISHING

Minneapolis, Minnesota

BEAR CLAW

Credits

Interior coloring by Jon Siruno.
Photos: 22T: © AP Photos/Anita Baca , 22B: Leif Skoogfors/FEMA.

Bearport Publishing
Minneapolis, MN
President: Jen Jenson
Director of Product Development: Spencer Brinker
Editor: Allison Juda

Produced by Shoreline Publishing Group LLC
Santa Barbara, California
Designer: Patty Kelley
Editorial Director: James Buckley Jr.

DISCLAIMER: This graphic story is a dramatization based on true events. It is intended to give the reader a sense of the narrative rather than a presentation of actual details as they occurred.

Library of Congress Cataloging-in-Publication Data

Names: Buckley, James, Jr., 1963– author. | LaCross, Kerstin, 1988-
    illustrator.
Title: Vanished in the hurricane : dolphin rescue! / by James Buckley Jr. ;
    illustrated by, Kerstin LaCross.
Description: Bear claw books. | Minneapolis, MN : Bearport Publishing,
    [2021] | Series: Rescued! Animal escapes | Includes bibliographical
    references and index.
Identifiers: LCCN 2020035454 (print) | LCCN 2020035455 (ebook) | ISBN
    9781647476205 (library binding) | ISBN 9781647476274 (paperback) | ISBN
    9781647476342 (ebook)
Subjects: LCSH: Captive dolphins—Mississippi—Gulfport—Juvenile
    literature. | Wildlife rescue—Mississippi—Gulfport—Juvenile
    literature. | Hurricane Katrina, 2005—Juvenile literature.
Classification: LCC SF408.6.D64 B83 2021 (print) | LCC SF408.6.D64
    (ebook) | DDC 636.95309762/13—dc23
LC record available at https://lccn.loc.gov/2020035454
LC ebook record available at https://lccn.loc.gov/2020035455

For more information, write to Bearport Publishing, 5357 Penn Avenue South, Minneapolis, MN 55419. Printed in the United States of America.

CONTENTS

CHAPTER 1

Blow, Winds, Blow!

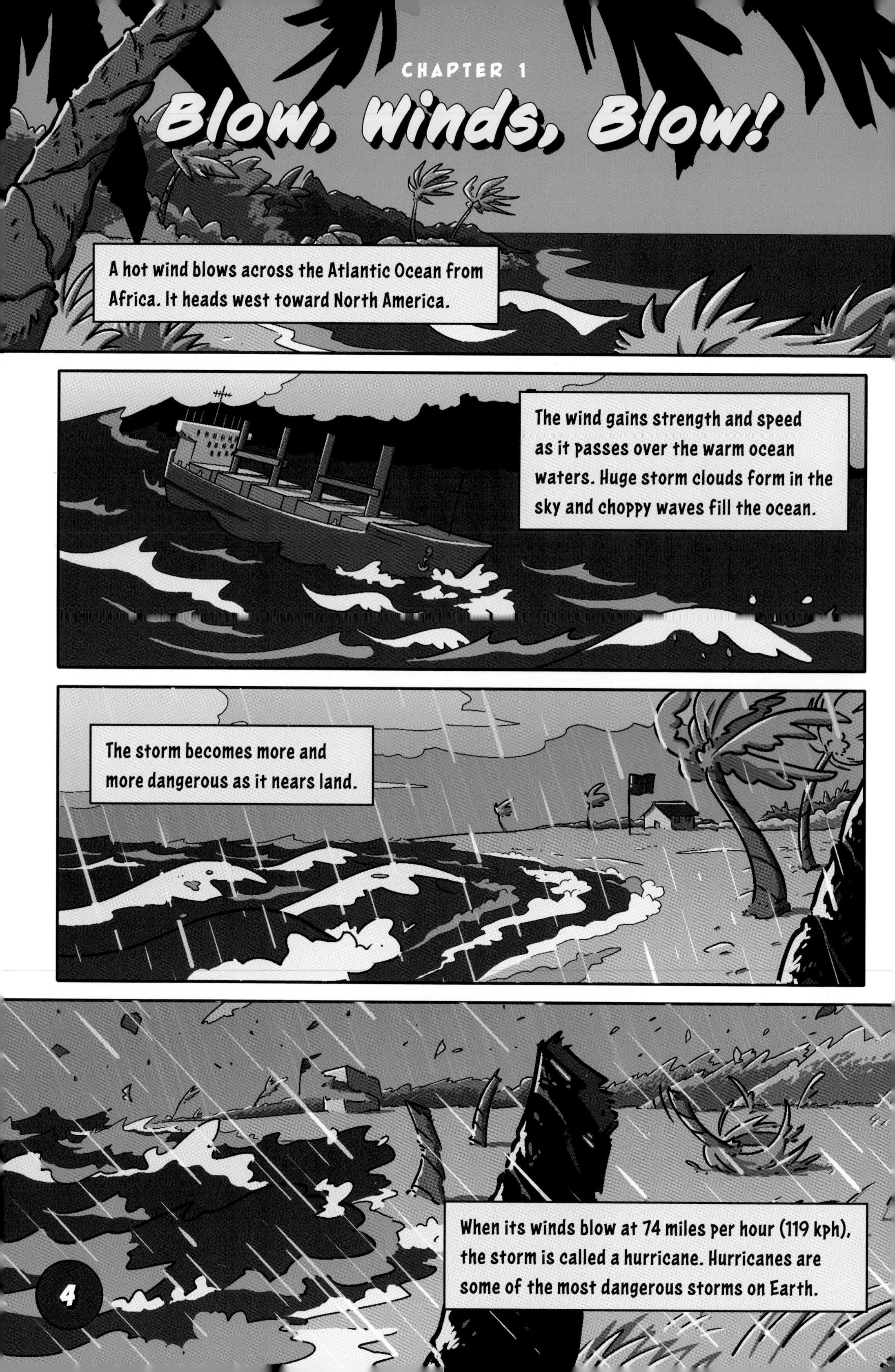
A hot wind blows across the Atlantic Ocean from Africa. It heads west toward North America.
The wind gains strength and speed as it passes over the warm ocean waters. Huge storm clouds form in the sky and choppy waves fill the ocean.
The storm becomes more and more dangerous as it nears land.
When its winds blow at 74 miles per hour (119 kph), the storm is called a hurricane. Hurricanes are some of the most dangerous storms on Earth.

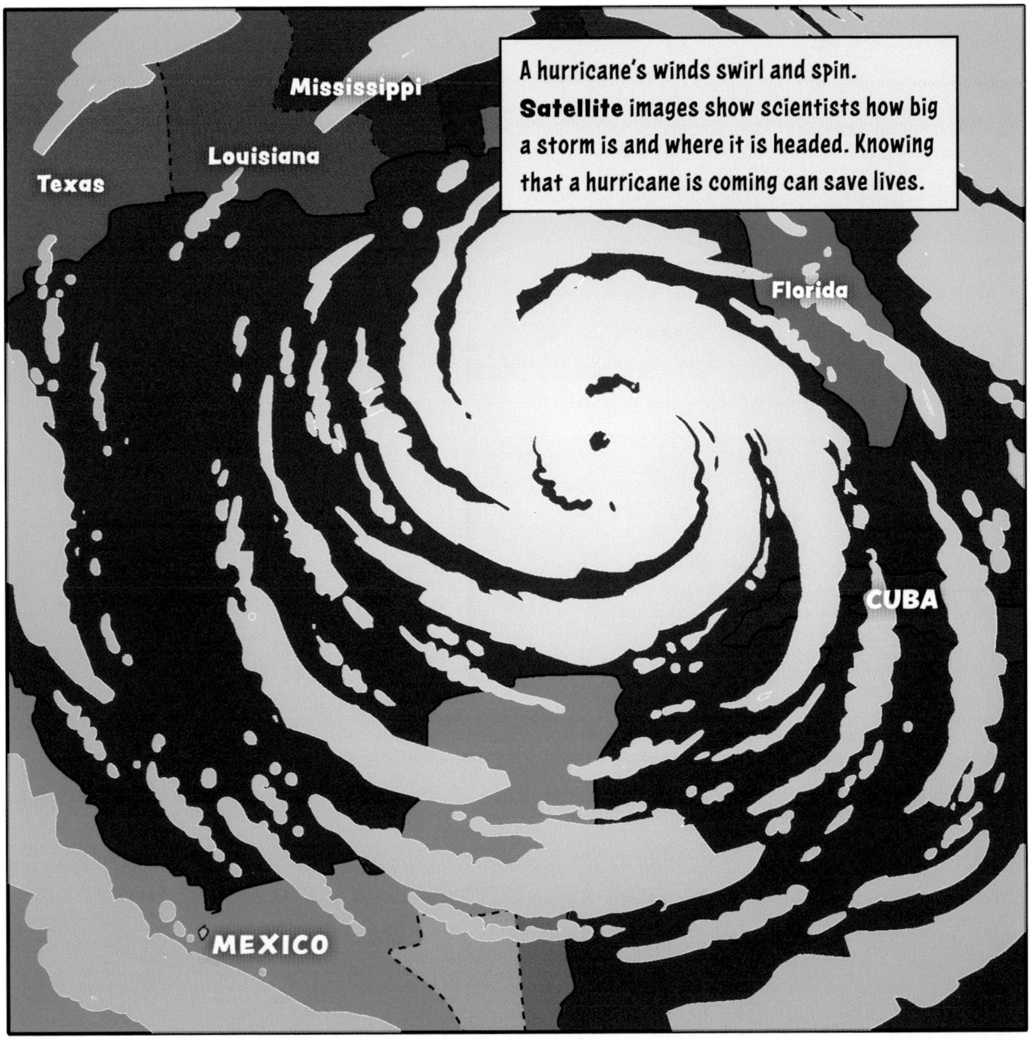
A hurricane's winds swirl and spin. **Satellite** images show scientists how big a storm is and where it is headed. Knowing that a hurricane is coming can save lives.
Mississippi
Louisiana
Texas
Florida
CUBA
MEXICO

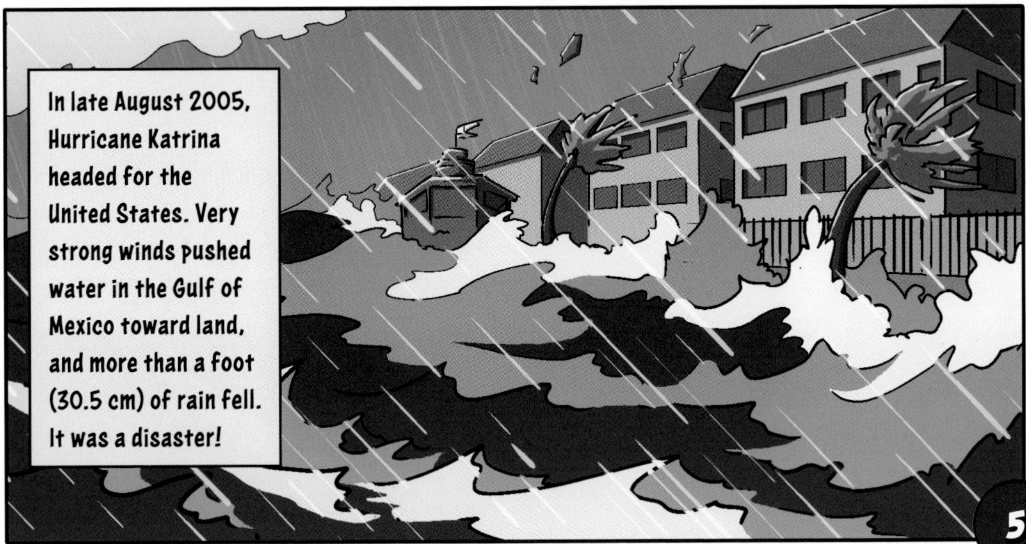
In late August 2005, Hurricane Katrina headed for the United States. Very strong winds pushed water in the Gulf of Mexico toward land, and more than a foot (30.5 cm) of rain fell. It was a disaster!

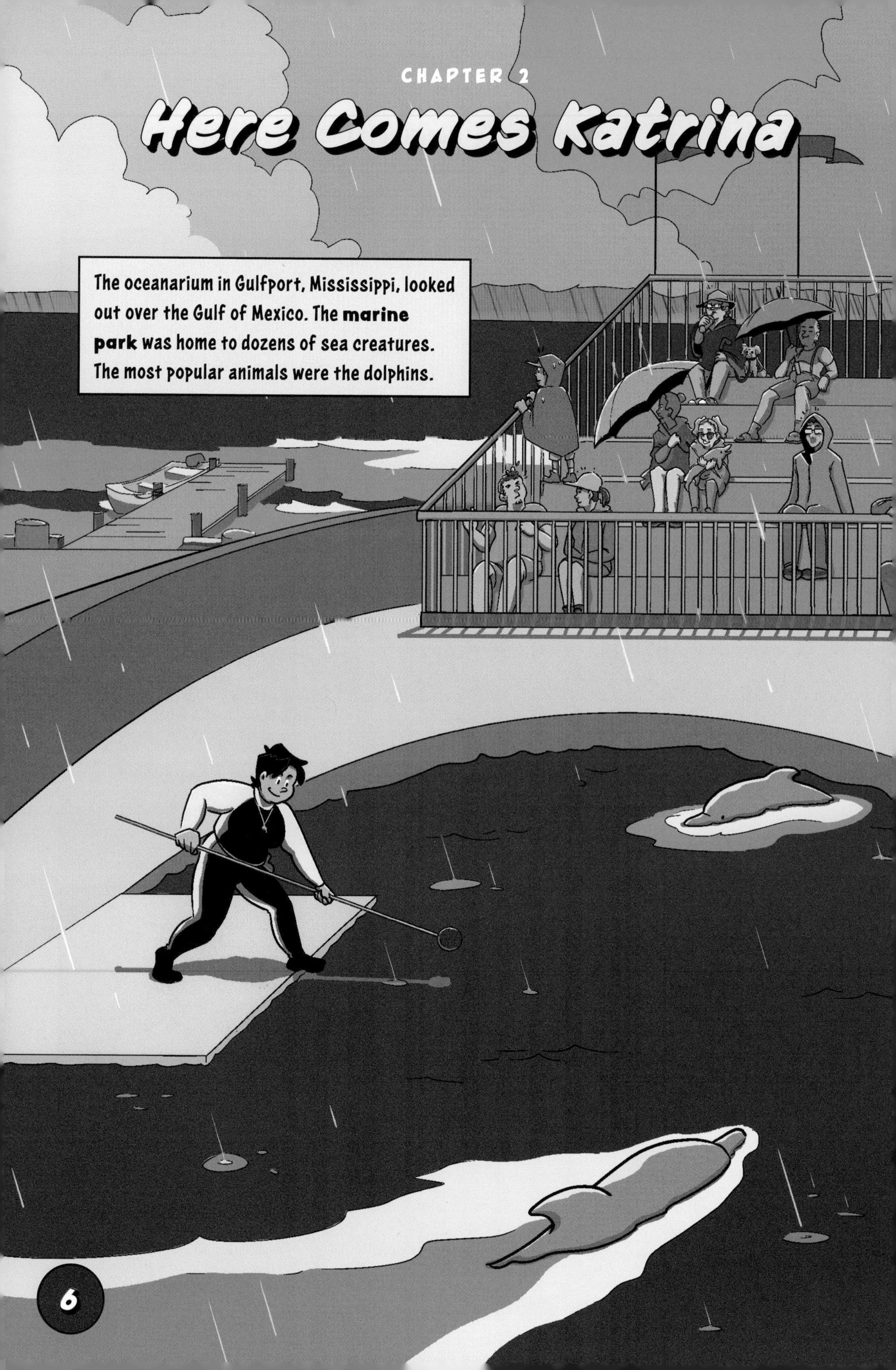
CHAPTER 2
Here Comes Katrina
The oceanarium in Gulfport, Mississippi, looked out over the Gulf of Mexico. The **marine park** was home to dozens of sea creatures. The most popular animals were the dolphins.

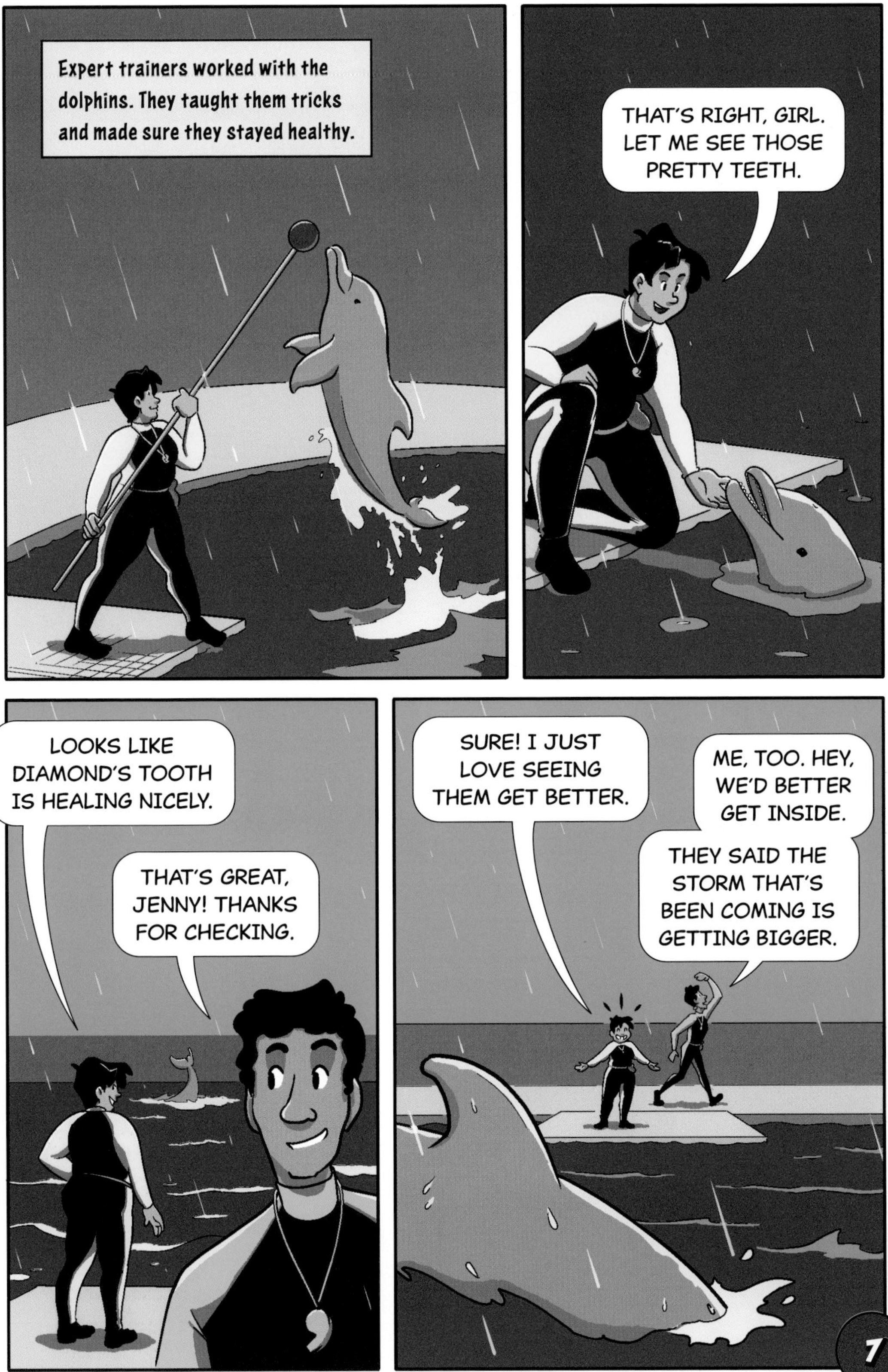
Expert trainers worked with the dolphins. They taught them tricks and made sure they stayed healthy.
THAT'S RIGHT, GIRL. LET ME SEE THOSE PRETTY TEETH.
LOOKS LIKE DIAMOND'S TOOTH IS HEALING NICELY.
THAT'S GREAT, JENNY! THANKS FOR CHECKING.
SURE! I JUST LOVE SEEING THEM GET BETTER.
ME, TOO. HEY, WE'D BETTER GET INSIDE.
THEY SAID THE STORM THAT'S BEEN COMING IS GETTING BIGGER.

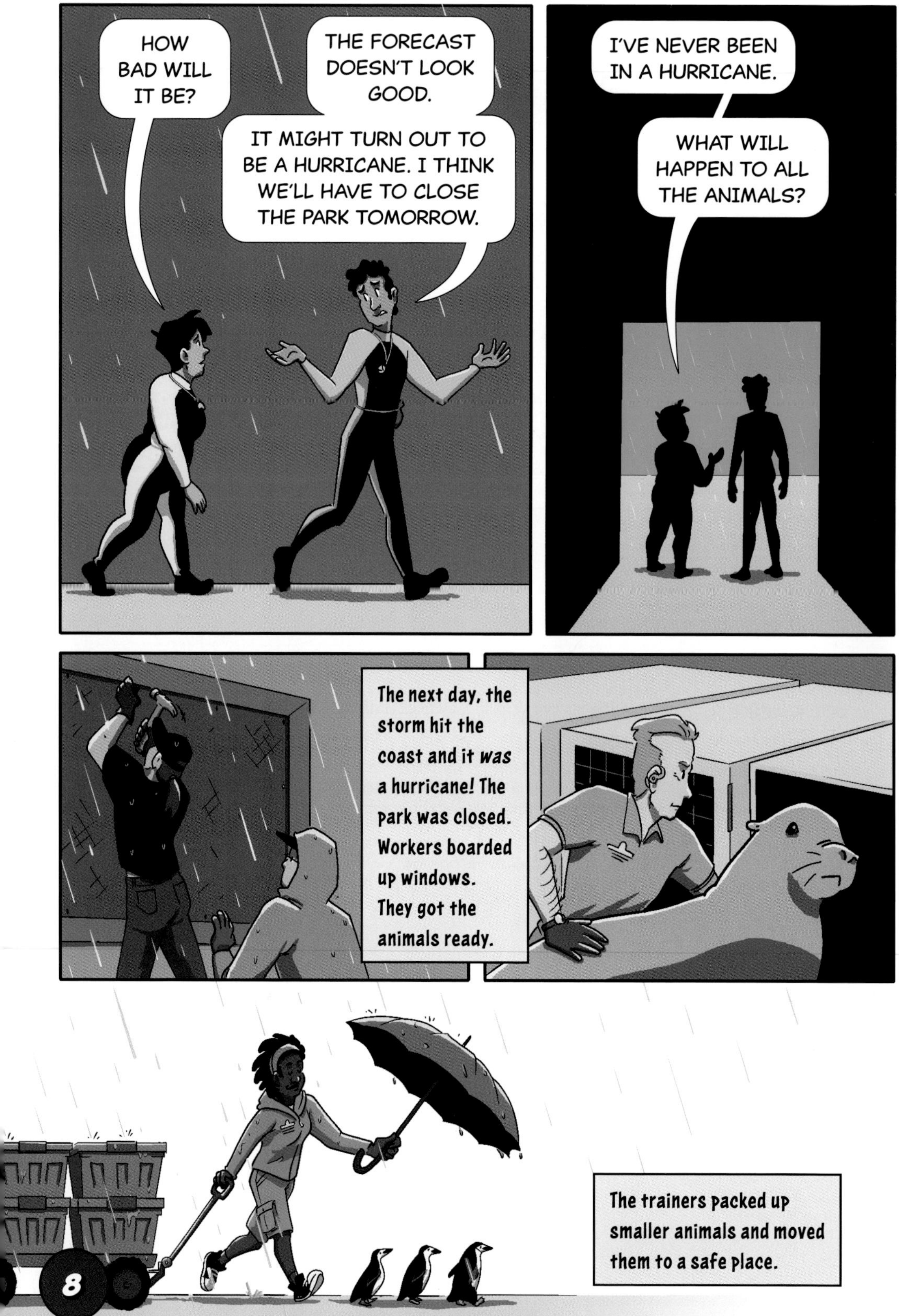
HOW BAD WILL IT BE?
THE FORECAST DOESN'T LOOK GOOD.
IT MIGHT TURN OUT TO BE A HURRICANE. I THINK WE'LL HAVE TO CLOSE THE PARK TOMORROW.
I'VE NEVER BEEN IN A HURRICANE.
WHAT WILL HAPPEN TO ALL THE ANIMALS?
The next day, the storm hit the coast and it *was* a hurricane! The park was closed. Workers boarded up windows. They got the animals ready.
The trainers packed up smaller animals and moved them to a safe place.

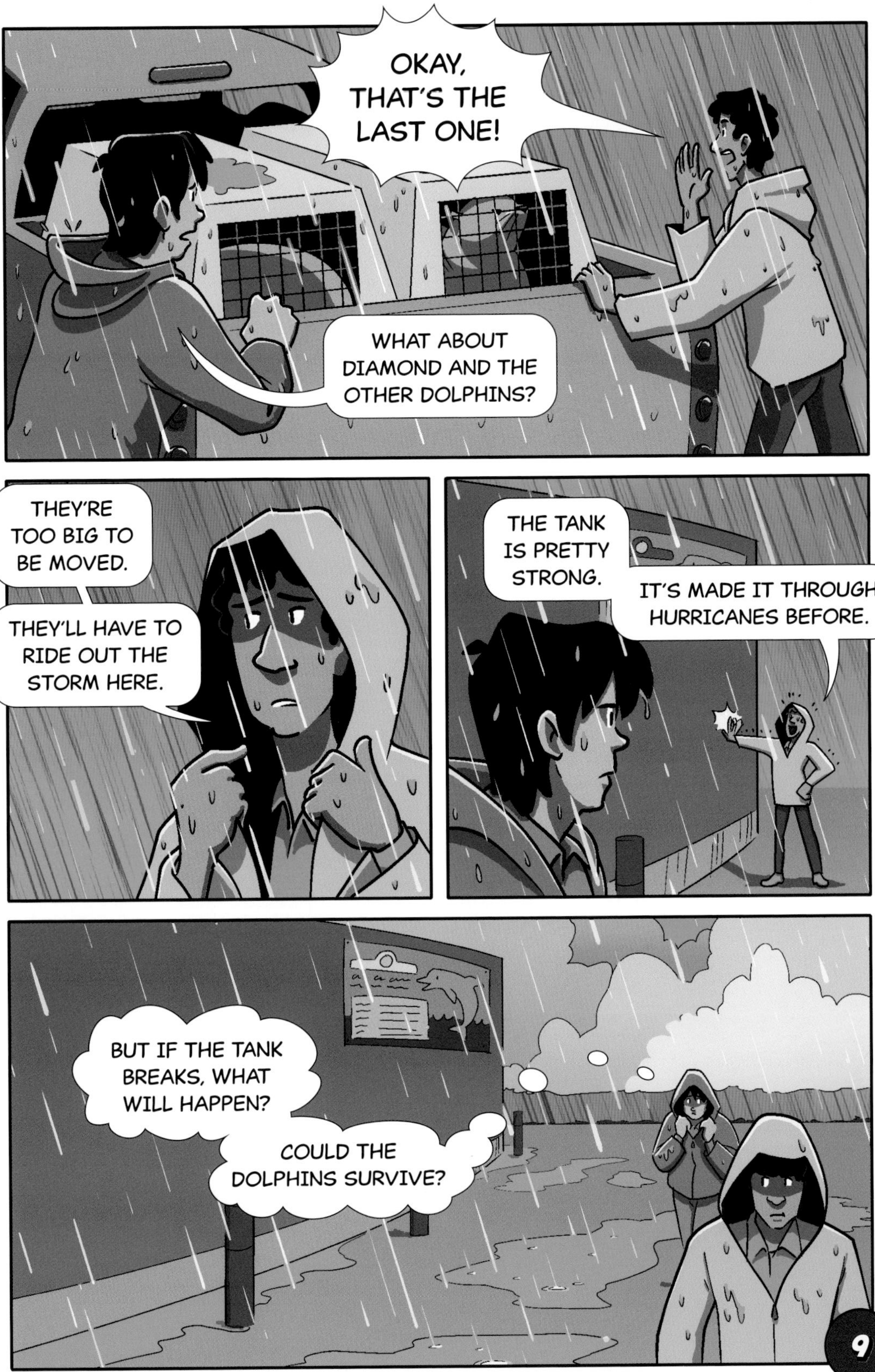
OKAY, THAT'S THE LAST ONE!
WHAT ABOUT DIAMOND AND THE OTHER DOLPHINS?
THEY'RE TOO BIG TO BE MOVED.
THEY'LL HAVE TO RIDE OUT THE STORM HERE.
THE TANK IS PRETTY STRONG.
IT'S MADE IT THROUGH HURRICANES BEFORE.
BUT IF THE TANK BREAKS, WHAT WILL HAPPEN?
COULD THE DOLPHINS SURVIVE?

CHAPTER 3
Washed Away

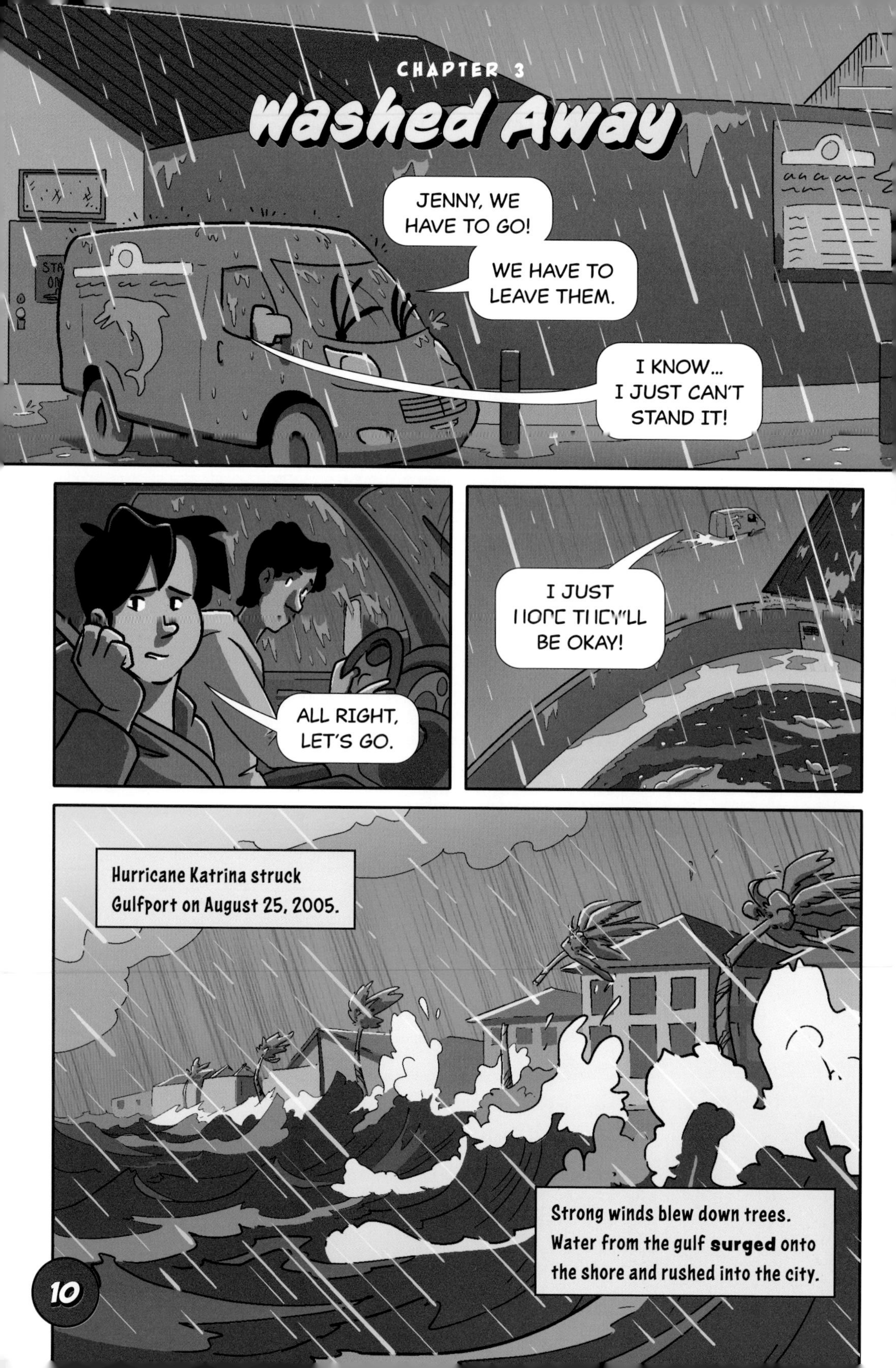

JENNY, WE HAVE TO GO!
WE HAVE TO LEAVE THEM.
I KNOW... I JUST CAN'T STAND IT!
ALL RIGHT, LET'S GO.
I JUST HOPE THEY'LL BE OKAY!
Hurricane Katrina struck Gulfport on August 25, 2005.
Strong winds blew down trees. Water from the gulf **surged** onto the shore and rushed into the city.

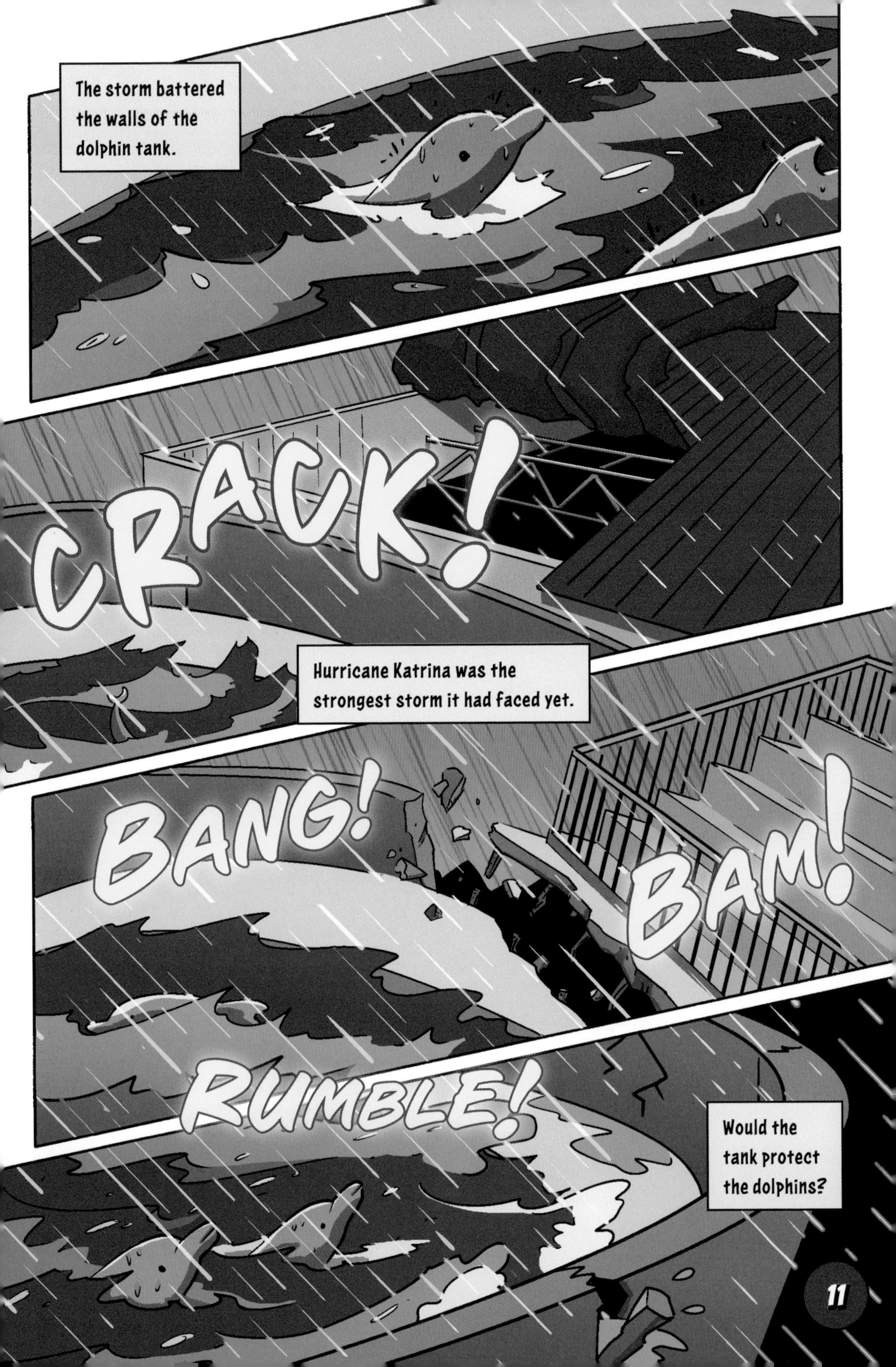

The storm battered the walls of the dolphin tank.
CRACK!
Hurricane Katrina was the strongest storm it had faced yet.
BANG!
BAM!
RUMBLE!
Would the tank protect the dolphins?

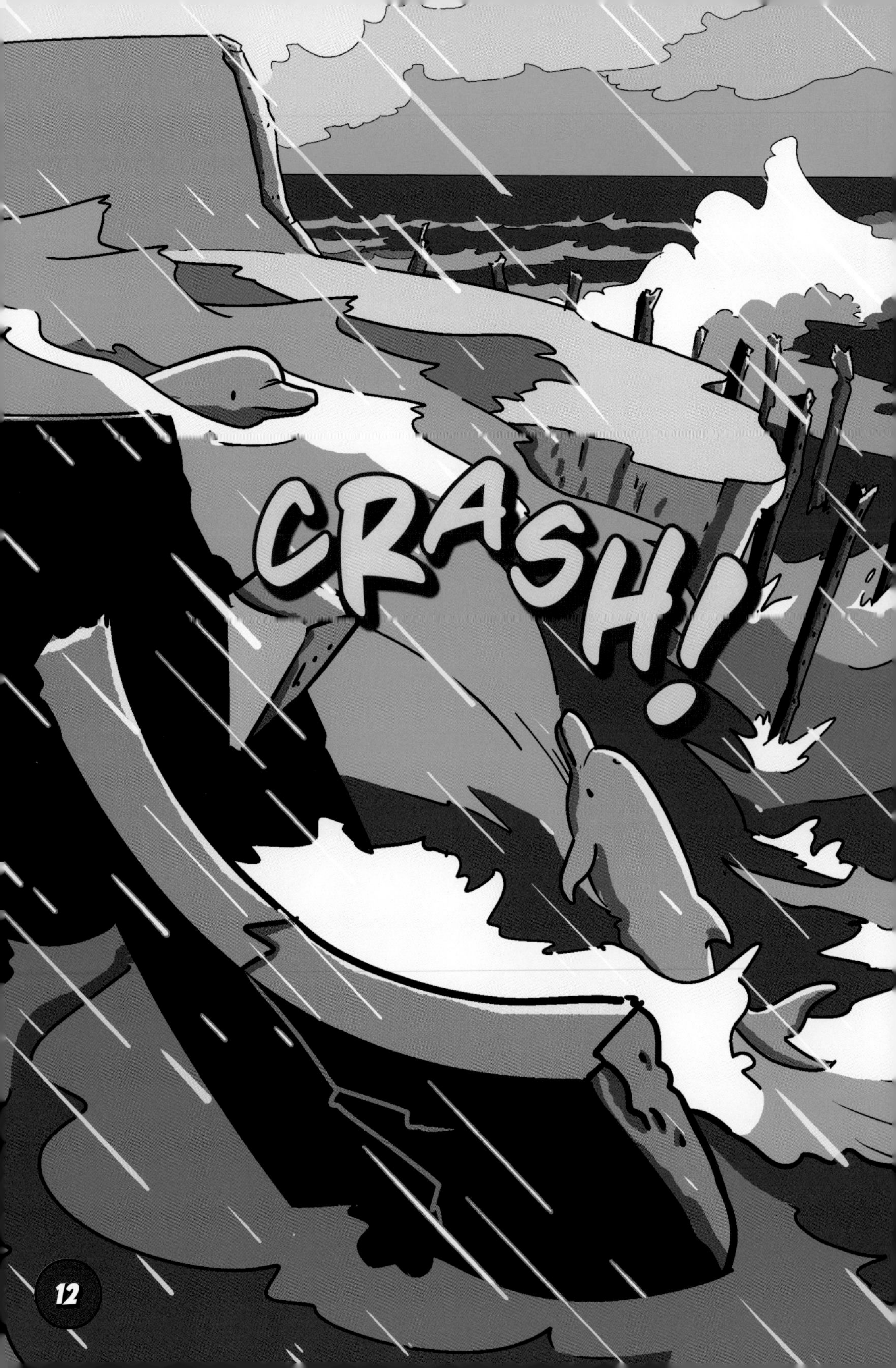
CRASH!

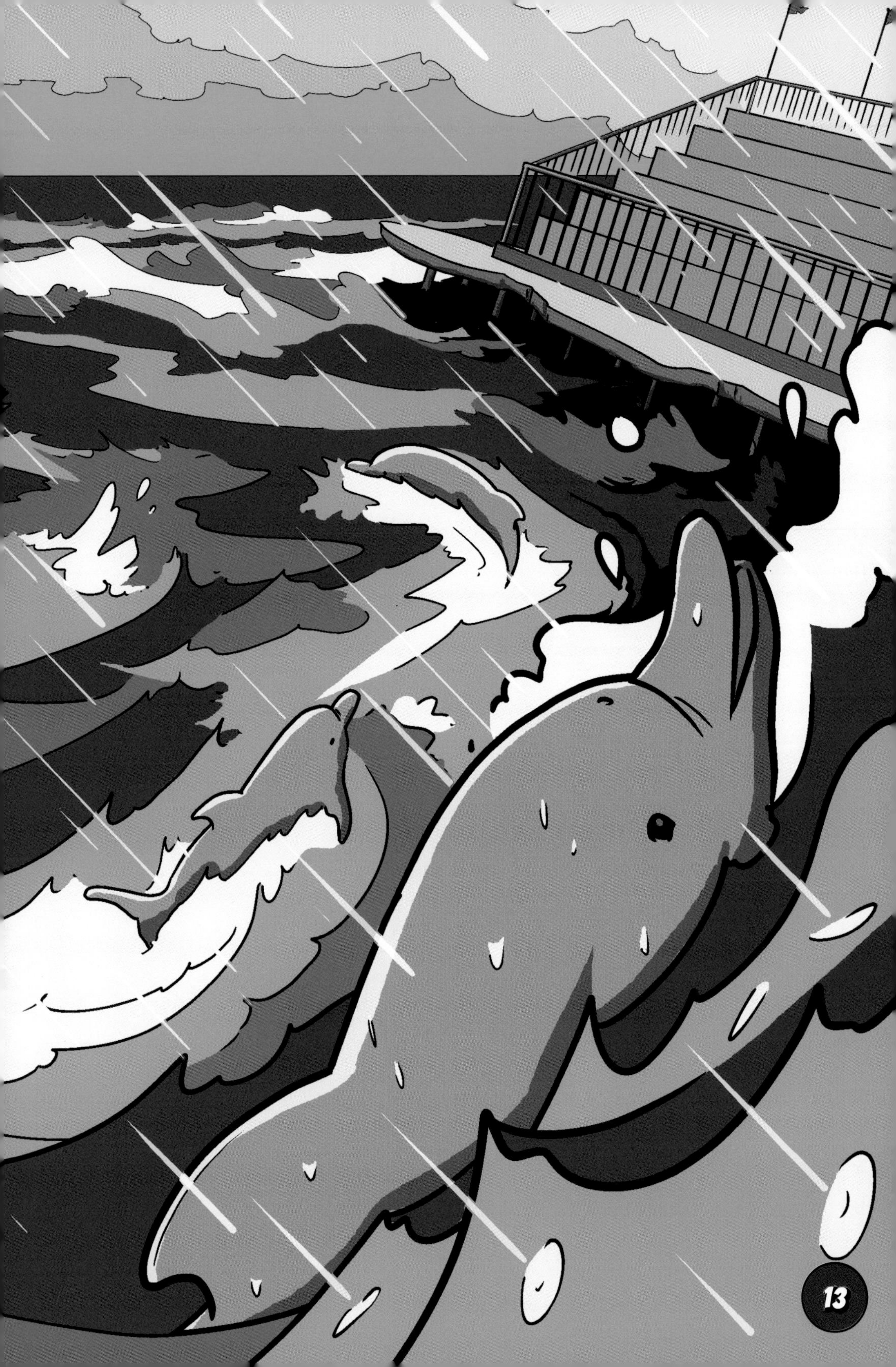

CHAPTER 4

Rescued!

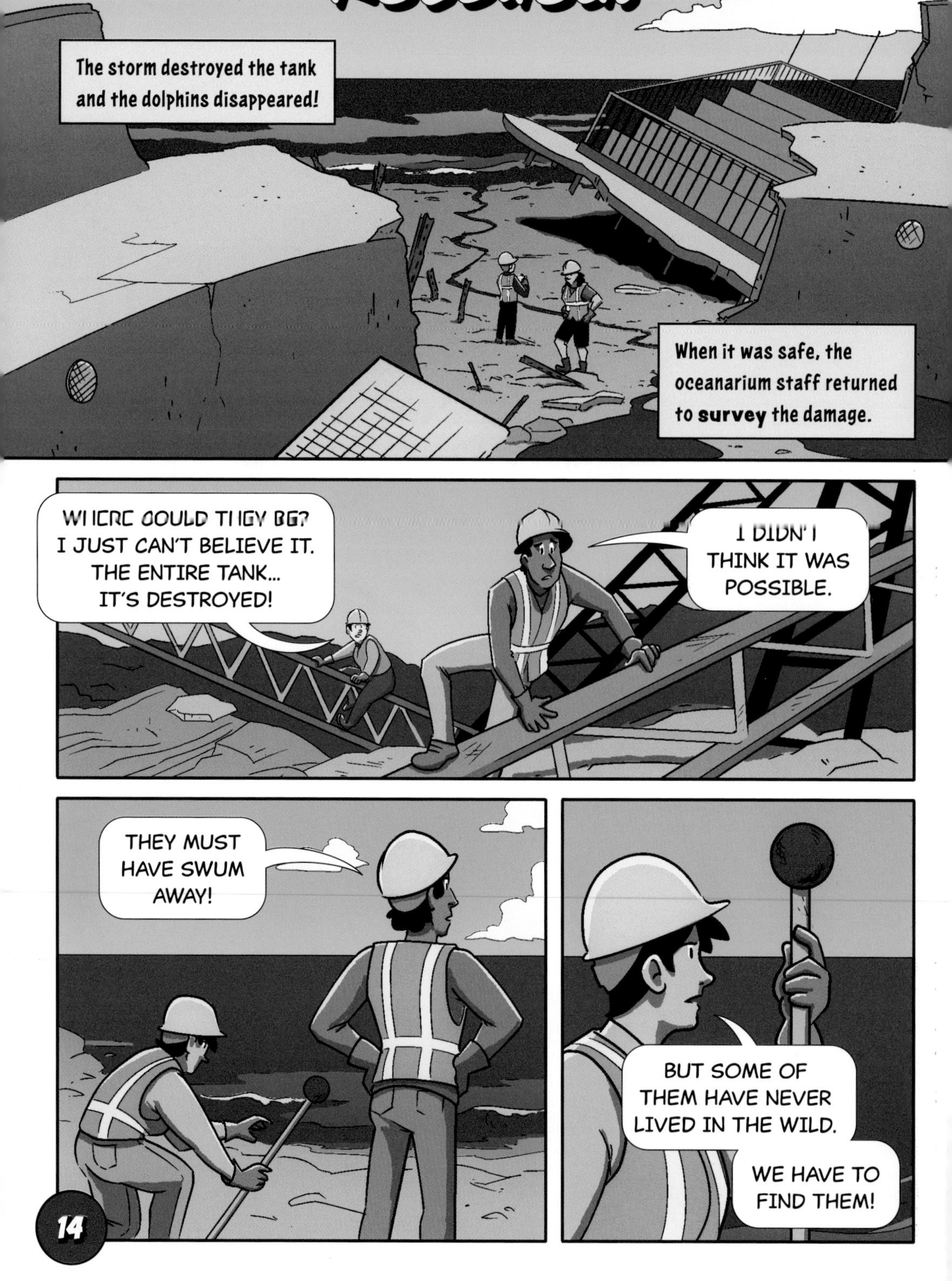

The storm destroyed the tank and the dolphins disappeared!
When it was safe, the oceanarium staff returned to **survey** the damage.
WHERE COULD THEY BE? I JUST CAN'T BELIEVE IT. THE ENTIRE TANK... IT'S DESTROYED!
I DIDN'T THINK IT WAS POSSIBLE.
THEY MUST HAVE SWUM AWAY!
BUT SOME OF THEM HAVE NEVER LIVED IN THE WILD.
WE HAVE TO FIND THEM!

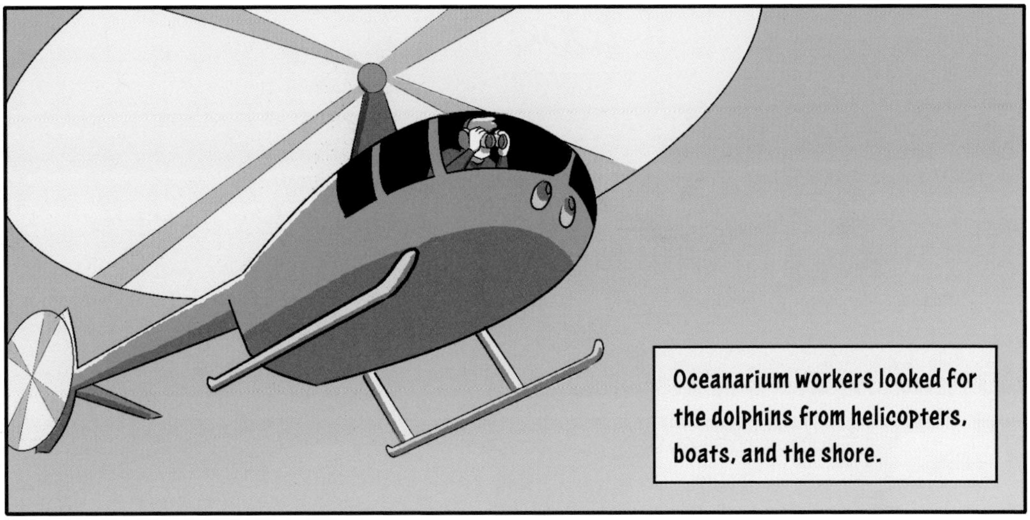
Oceanarium workers looked for the dolphins from helicopters, boats, and the shore.

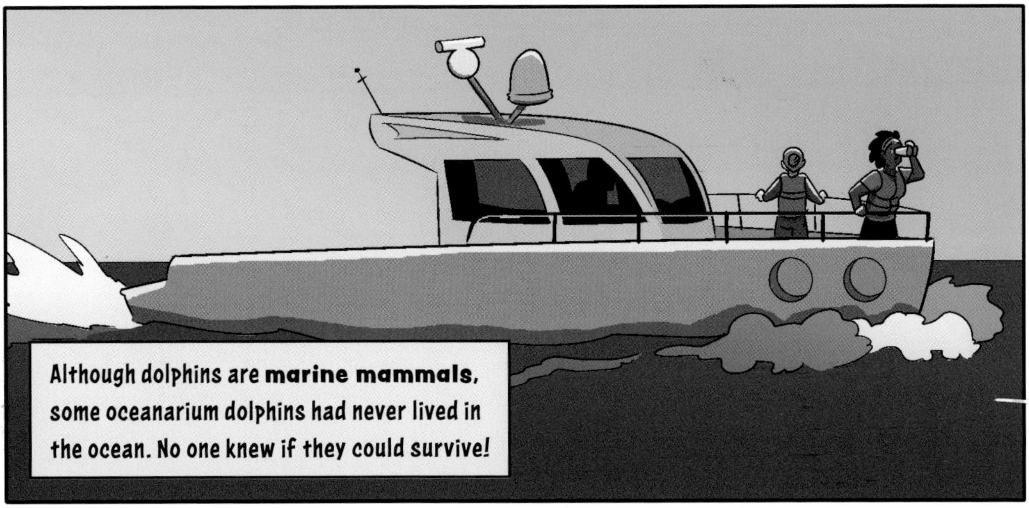
Although dolphins are **marine mammals**, some oceanarium dolphins had never lived in the ocean. No one knew if they could survive!

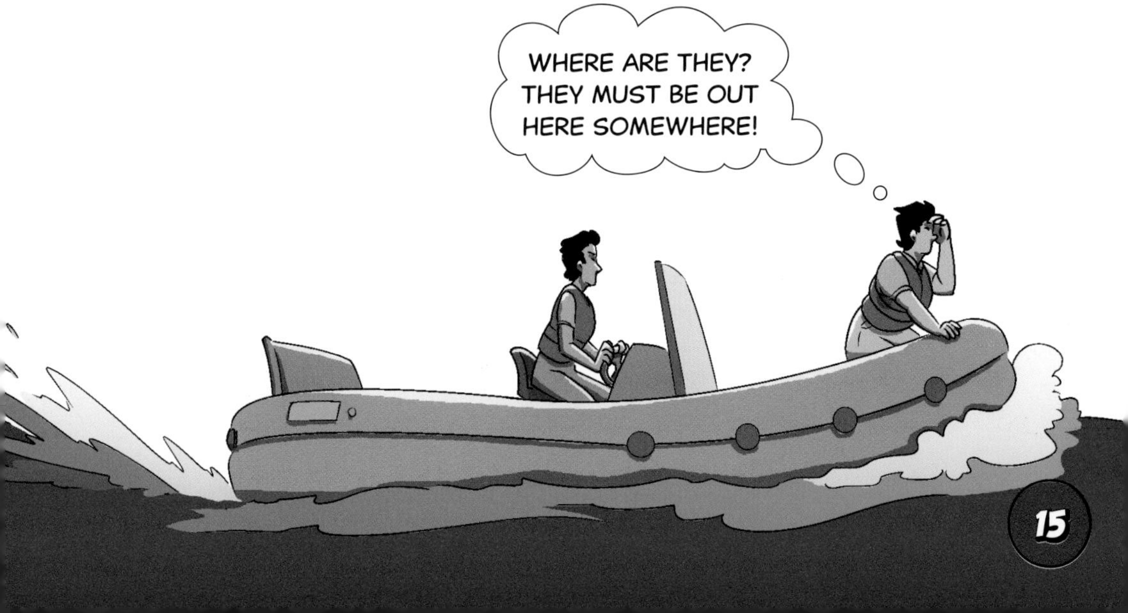
WHERE ARE THEY? THEY MUST BE OUT HERE SOMEWHERE!

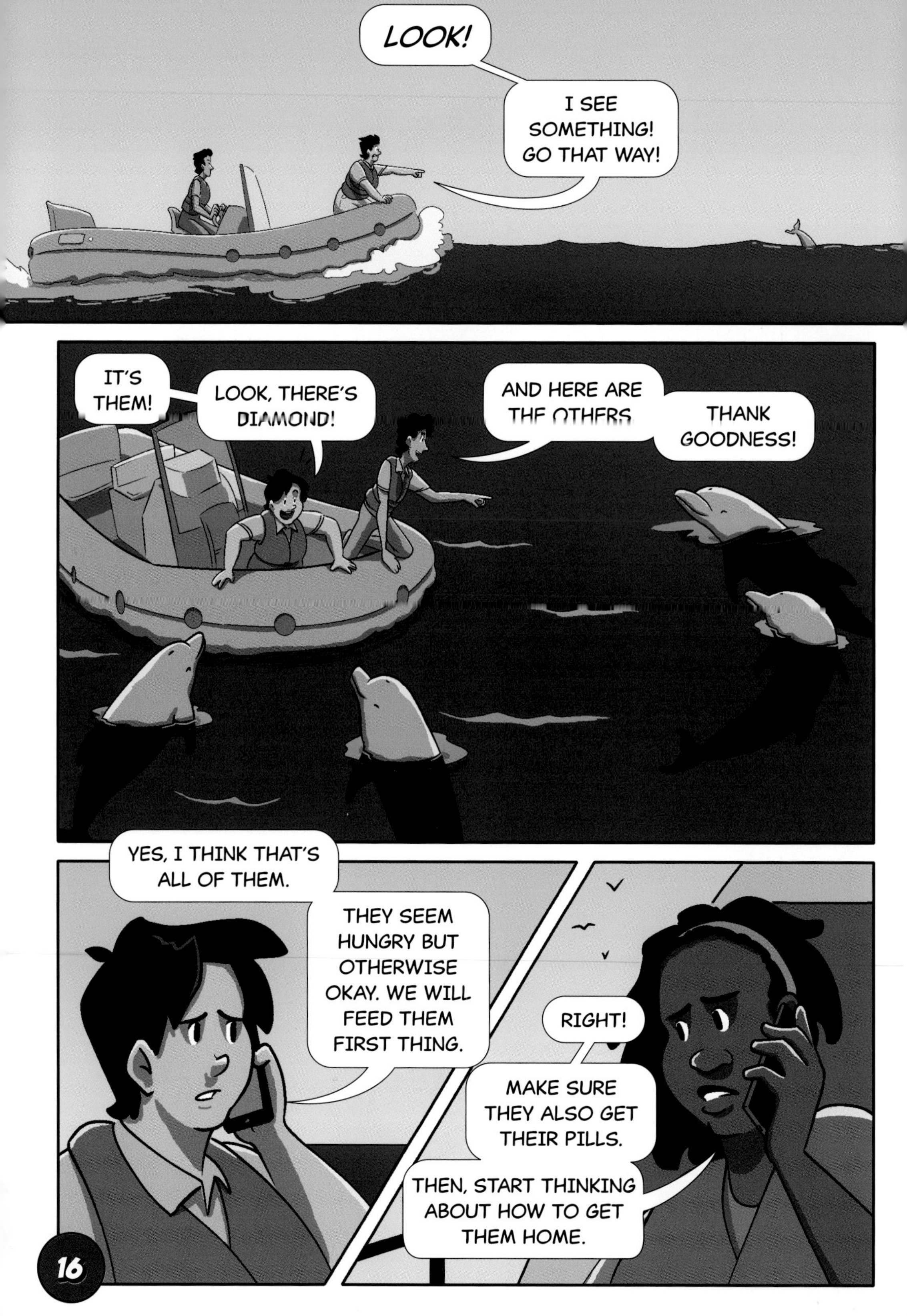

LOOK!
I SEE SOMETHING! GO THAT WAY!
IT'S THEM!
LOOK, THERE'S DIAMOND!
AND HERE ARE THE OTHERS.
THANK GOODNESS!
YES, I THINK THAT'S ALL OF THEM.
THEY SEEM HUNGRY BUT OTHERWISE OKAY. WE WILL FEED THEM FIRST THING.
RIGHT!
MAKE SURE THEY ALSO GET THEIR PILLS.
THEN, START THINKING ABOUT HOW TO GET THEM HOME.

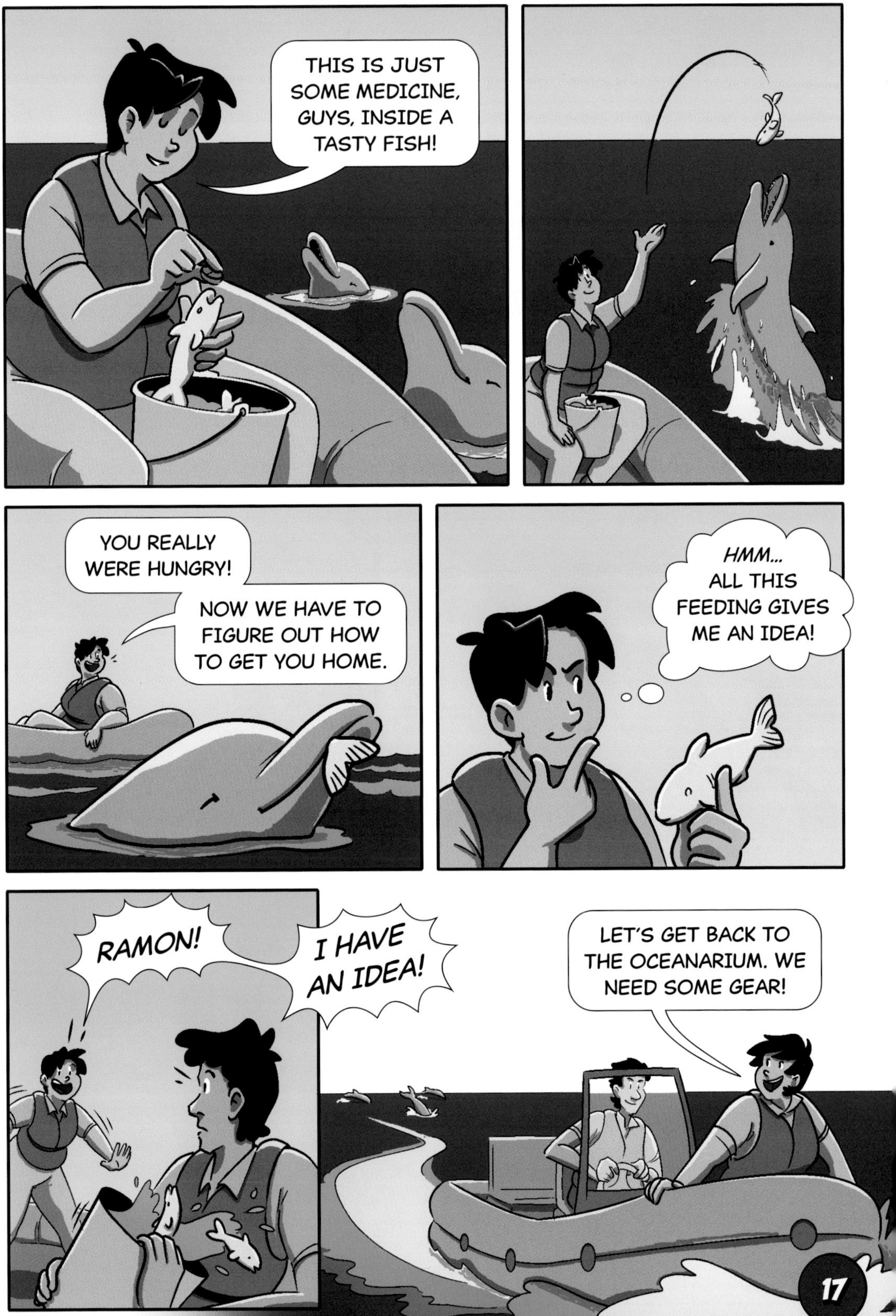
THIS IS JUST SOME MEDICINE, GUYS, INSIDE A TASTY FISH!
YOU REALLY WERE HUNGRY!
NOW WE HAVE TO FIGURE OUT HOW TO GET YOU HOME.
HMM... ALL THIS FEEDING GIVES ME AN IDEA!
RAMON!
I HAVE AN IDEA!
LET'S GET BACK TO THE OCEANARIUM. WE NEED SOME GEAR!

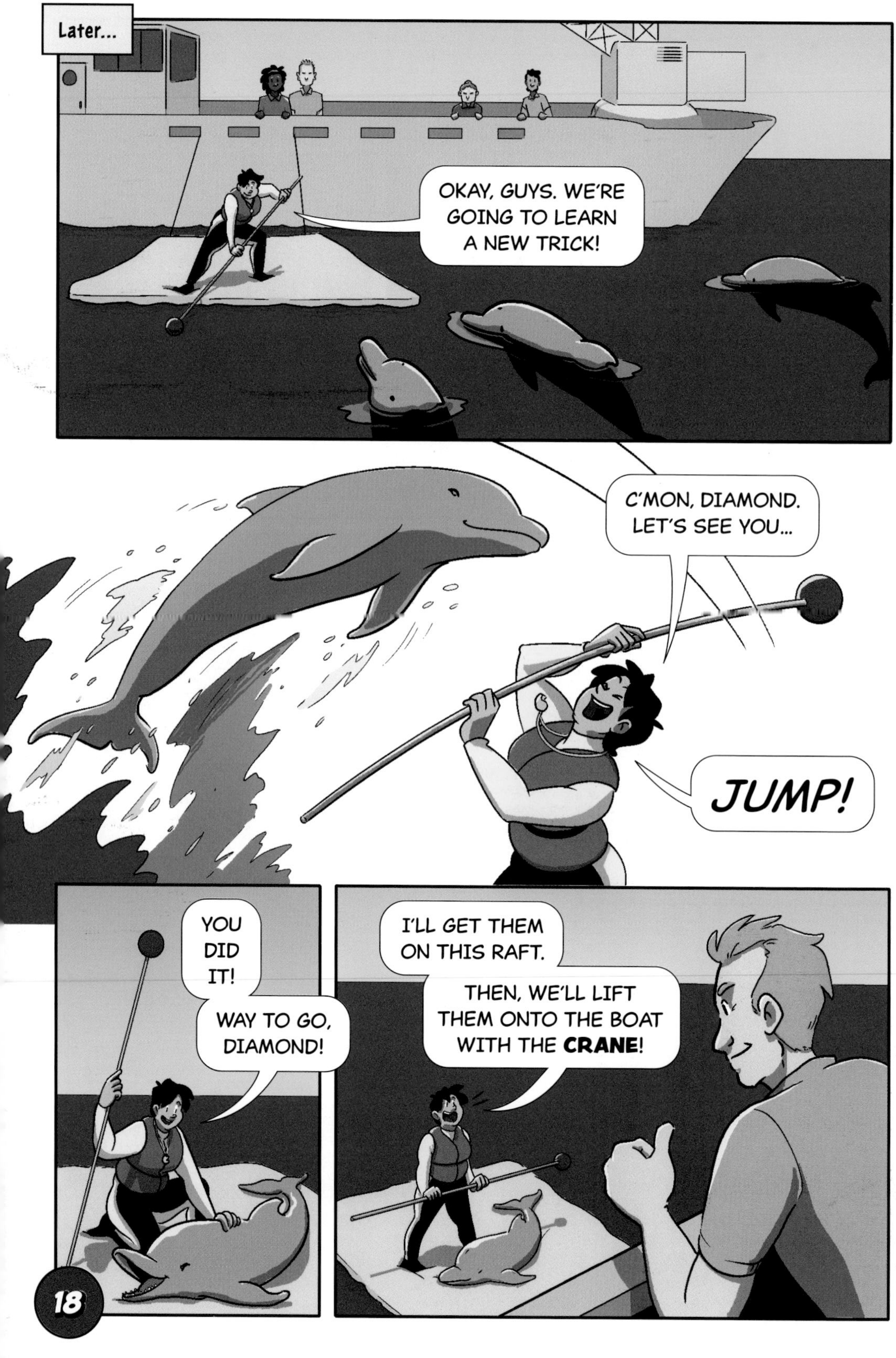
Later...
OKAY, GUYS. WE'RE GOING TO LEARN A NEW TRICK!
C'MON, DIAMOND. LET'S SEE YOU...
JUMP!
YOU DID IT!
WAY TO GO, DIAMOND!
I'LL GET THEM ON THIS RAFT.
THEN, WE'LL LIFT THEM ONTO THE BOAT WITH THE **CRANE**!

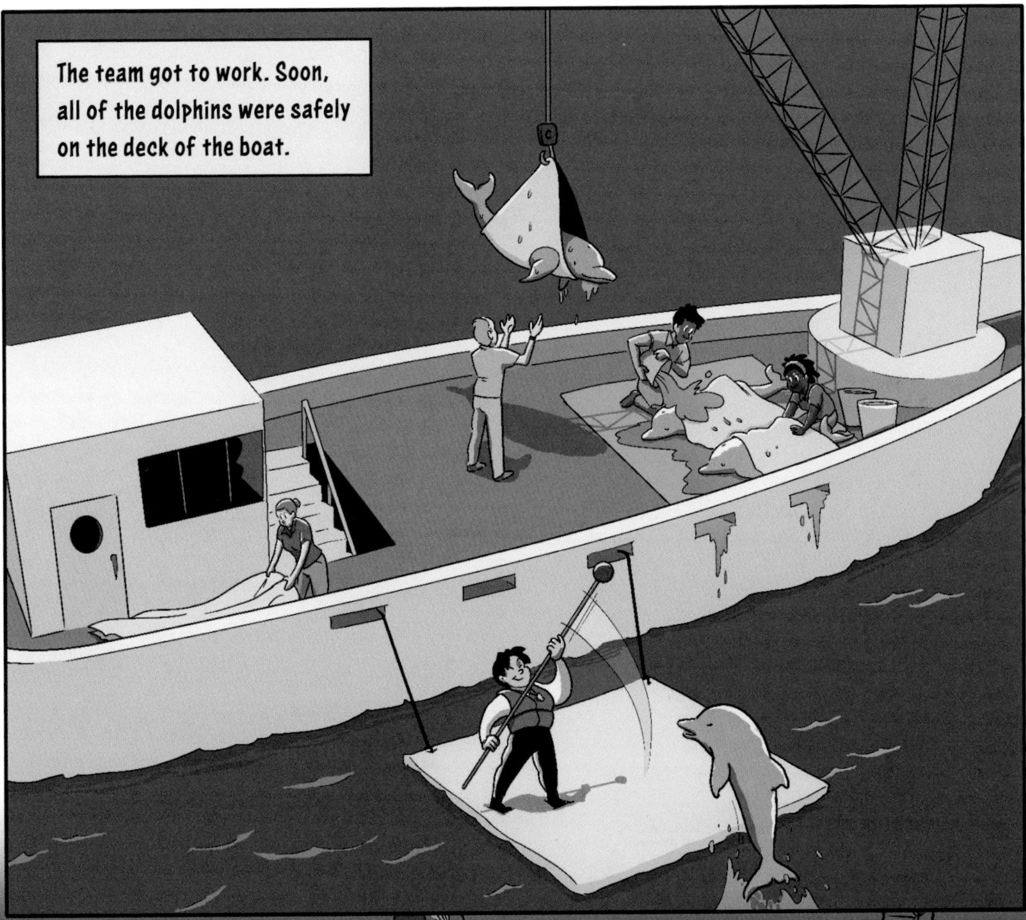
The team got to work. Soon, all of the dolphins were safely on the deck of the boat.

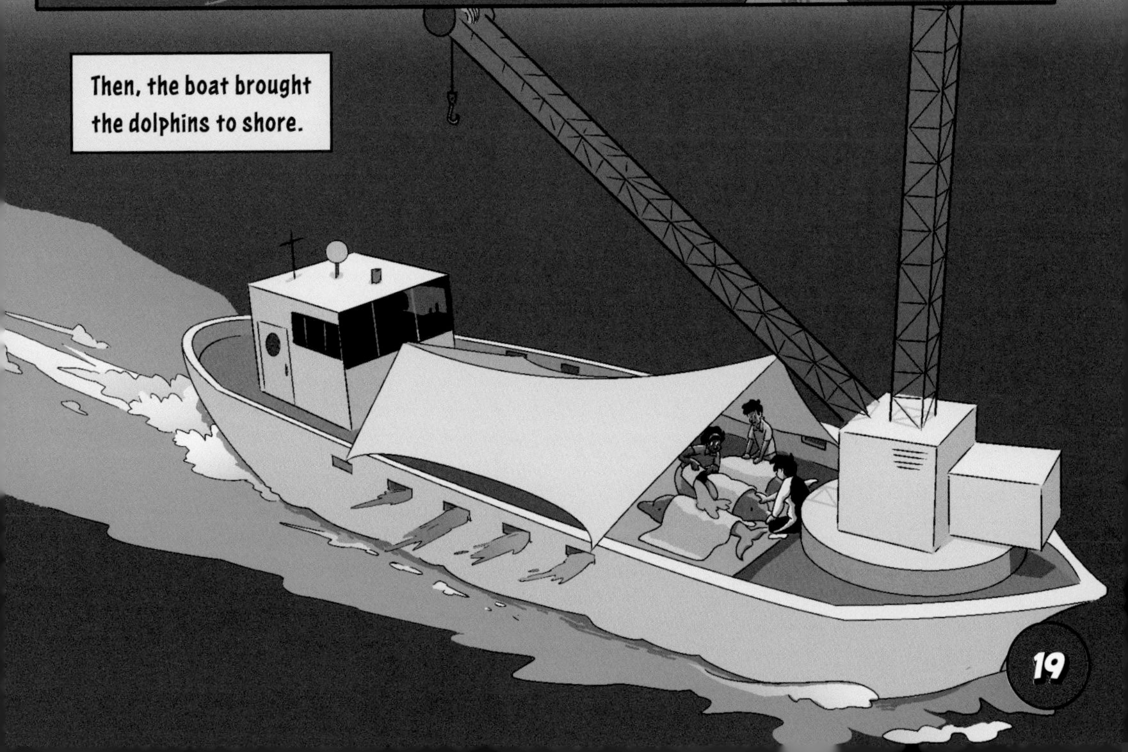
Then, the boat brought the dolphins to shore.

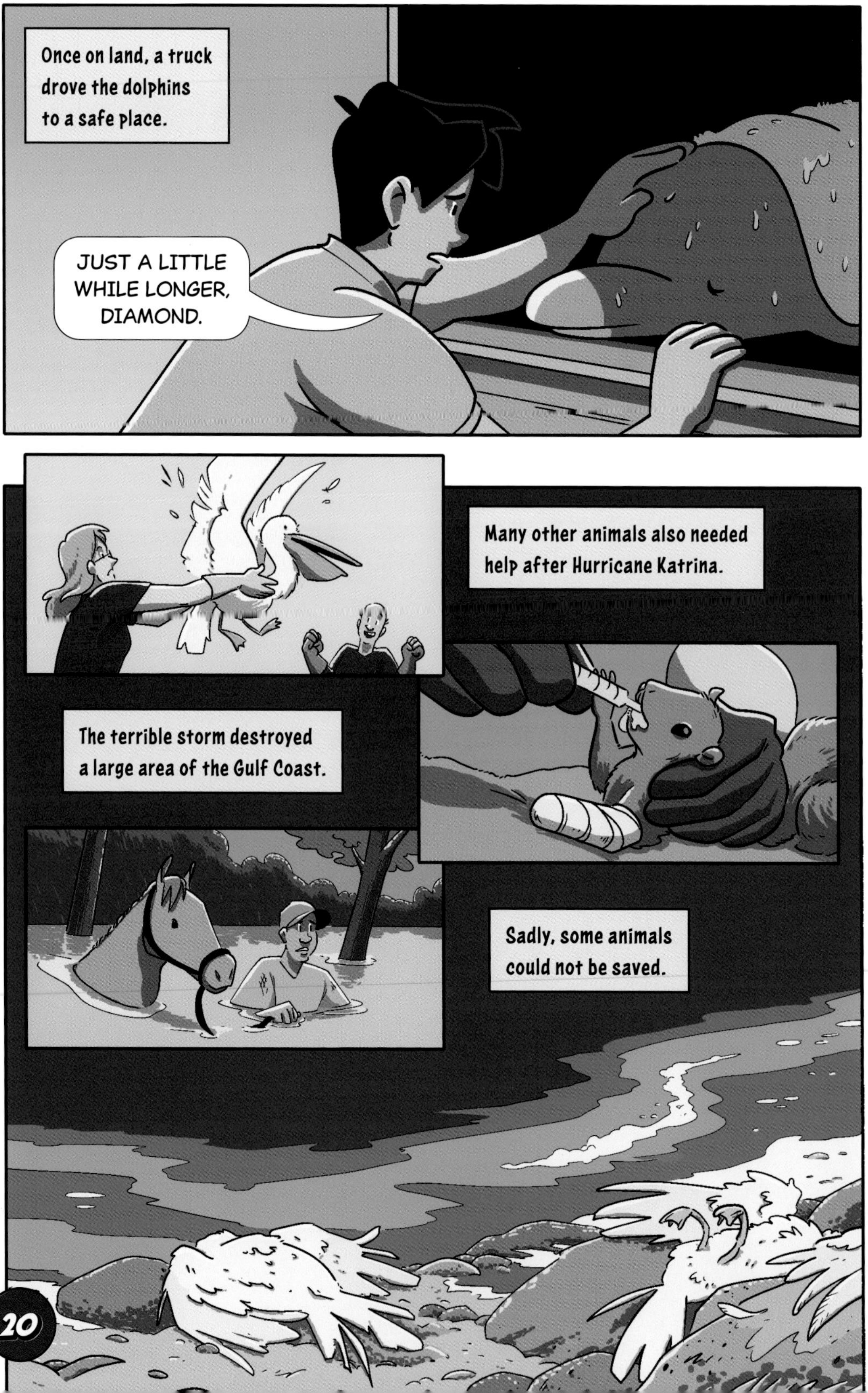
Once on land, a truck drove the dolphins to a safe place.
JUST A LITTLE WHILE LONGER, DIAMOND.
Many other animals also needed help after Hurricane Katrina.
The terrible storm destroyed a large area of the Gulf Coast.
Sadly, some animals could not be saved.

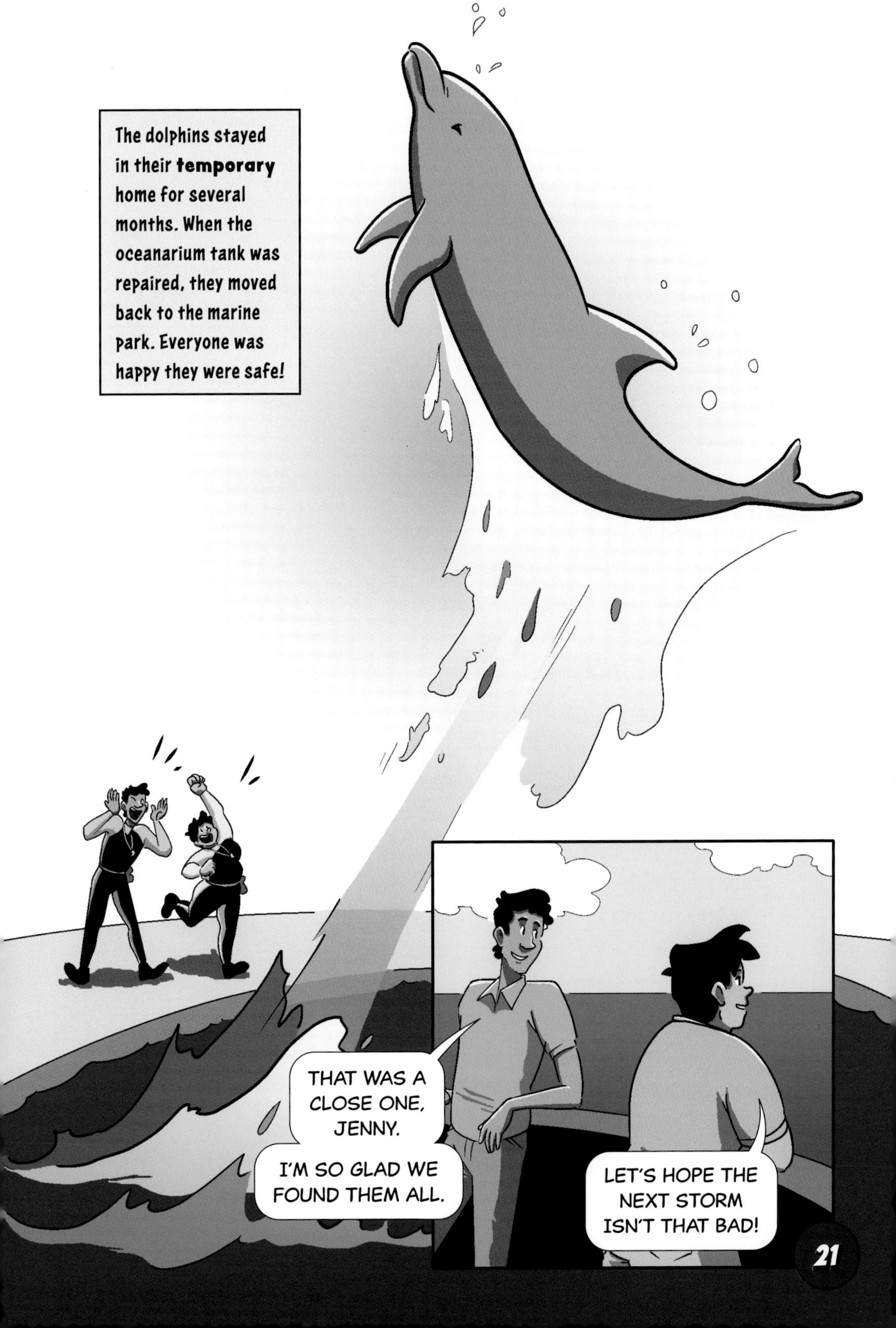
The dolphins stayed in their **temporary** home for several months. When the oceanarium tank was repaired, they moved back to the marine park. Everyone was happy they were safe!
THAT WAS A CLOSE ONE, JENNY.
I'M SO GLAD WE FOUND THEM ALL.
LET'S HOPE THE NEXT STORM ISN'T THAT BAD!

OTHER
HURRICANE RESCUES

HURRICANE MITCH

In October 1998, Hurricane Mitch hit
Central America. The storm killed
about 11,000 people and more than
50,000 animals. Many more were hurt.
The World Society for the Protection
of Animals raced to Central America to
help animals in danger. **Veterinarians**

traveled through areas hit by the storm to treat
horses, cows, and other animals. Volunteers moved
animals away from flooded areas. The animals were
given food, fresh water, and a safe place to live.

HURRICANE IKE

In September 2008, **meteorologists**
warned that a massive storm called
Hurricane Ike was moving toward
the coast of Texas. People began
to **evacuate** coastal areas, but
many animals were left behind. The
Society for the Prevention of Cruelty

to Animals in Houston helped lead an animal
rescue effort. Before the storm hit, the organization
evacuated 300 dogs, 400 cats, and 60 horses to
safe shelters. After the hurricane, volunteers cared
for more than 1,000 animals, including zoo animals
and wild animals.

GLOSSARY

crane a machine with a lifting arm

evacuate to leave a dangerous place or to remove people or animals from a dangerous place

marine mammals warm-blooded animals that live in water and drink milk from their mothers as babies

marine park a place where sea animals are cared for and put on display for the public

meteorologists scientists who study weather

satellite a spacecraft that orbits Earth and sends back information

surged raised and rushed quickly, such as the movement of water onto land

survey to look closely at an area of land

temporary not designed to last long or be permanent

veterinarians doctors who care for animals

INDEX

READ MORE

Cazenove, Christophe. *Armed and Dangerous (Sea Creatures #2).* New York: Papercutz, 2017.

Dickmann, Nancy. *Preparing for Severe Weather (Smithsonian Little Explorer: Little Meteorologist).* Washington, D.C.: Smithsonian Little Explorer, 2020.

McGregor, Harriet. *Destroyed by a Hurricane! (Uncharted: Stories of Survival).* Minneapolis: Bearport Publishing, 2021.

LEARN MORE ONLINE

1. Go to **www.factsurfer.com**
2. Enter "**Vanished in Hurricane**" into the search box.
3. Click on the cover of this book to see a list of websites.